5/13

BLAZERS

THE WORLD OF DRAGONS

THE ANATOMY OF A DRAGON

BY MATT DOEDEN

READING CONSULTANT:
BARBARA J. FOX
PROFESSOR EMERITA
NORTH CAROLINA STATE UNIVERSITY

CAPSTONE PRESS

Blazers Books are published by Capstone Press,
1710 Roe Crest Drive, North Mankato, Minnesota 56003
www.capstonepub.com

Library of Congress Cataloging-in-Publication Data
Cataloging-in-publication information is on file with the Library of Congress.
ISBN 978-1-62065-145-2 (library binding)
ISBN 978-1-4765-1377-5 (ebook PDF)

Editorial Credits
Aaron Sautter, editor; Kyle Grenz, designer; Eric Gohl, media researcher;
Jennifer Walker, production specialist

Photo Credits
Capstone: Federico Piatti, 13, Jonathan Mayer, 4–5, 6, 10–11, 21, 22, 26–27, 28, Krista Ward & Tod
Smith, 9 (bottom), 19, 29 (inset); Shutterstock: Algol, 9 (top), 16–17, lineartestpilot, 25, Patalakha
Serg, cover, Ulrich Willmunder, 29 (dragon), Unholy Vault Designs, cover (background), 1,
Willyam Bradberry, 14–15

Design Elements
Shutterstock

Printed in the United States of America in Brainerd, Minnesota.
092012   006938BANGS13

TABLE OF CONTENTS

A DEADLY DUEL

A knight waits in a moonlit field.
Soon a huge dragon appears in the sky.
The monster blasts a stream of fire at the
knight. But the knight blocks the flames
with his dragon scale shield.

knight—a warrior of the Middle Ages (AD 400–1500)
who wore armor and fought with a sword

scale—one of the small hard plates that covers the skin
of some reptiles

The knight jabs his spear at the dragon. But it bounces off the dragon's tough scales. The dragon slashes the knight with its claws. The knight falls to the ground in pain. The dragon then flies off to look for a tasty meal.

People who fight dragons often use shields made from dragon scales. These shields can resist both dragon fire and dragon magic.

SUPER SENSES

Dragons are imaginary creatures in stories and myths. Dragons have amazing senses. Their sense of smell is very strong. Jacobson's organs allow dragons to smell very faint odors.

myth—a story told long ago that many people believed to be true

Jacobson's organ—an odor-detecting organ inside the mouths of some reptiles

Jacobson's organ

DRAGON FACT

It is almost impossible to sneak up on dragons. Their strong senses usually warn them when enemies get too close.

Dragons have an incredible sense of touch. Their huge bodies can feel tiny vibrations in the ground. Dragons often feel something moving in their lairs before they see it.

vibration—a fast movement back and forth

lair—a place where a wild animal lives and sleeps

Eyesight is a dragon's strongest sense. Dragons can see things moving from great distances. Their sharp eyesight makes dragons great hunters and dangerous enemies.

Dragons have magical powers in many stories. They cast spells to protect their treasure or to control people's minds.

13

FANTASTIC FLYERS

Most dragons would seem too huge to fly. But they do anyway. Some flying dragons store gas in their bodies. The gas is lighter than air. It helps lift dragons' large bodies so they can fly.

DRAGON FACT

Not all dragons can fly. Some have small, useless wings. Others have no wings at all.

15

Most dragons have streamlined bodies that help them reach great speeds while flying.

Huge dragons may also be able to fly because of their bones. Dragon bones are strong and hollow like a bird's. A dragon's strong, lightweight skeleton helps support its body while flying.

skeleton—the bones that support and protect the body of an animal

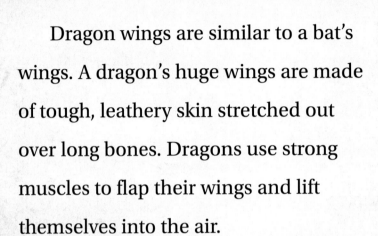

Dragon wings are similar to a bat's wings. A dragon's huge wings are made of tough, leathery skin stretched out over long bones. Dragons use strong muscles to flap their wings and lift themselves into the air.

DRAGON FACT

In some stories from China and Japan, dragons can fly without wings. These snakelike dragons soar through the air using magic.

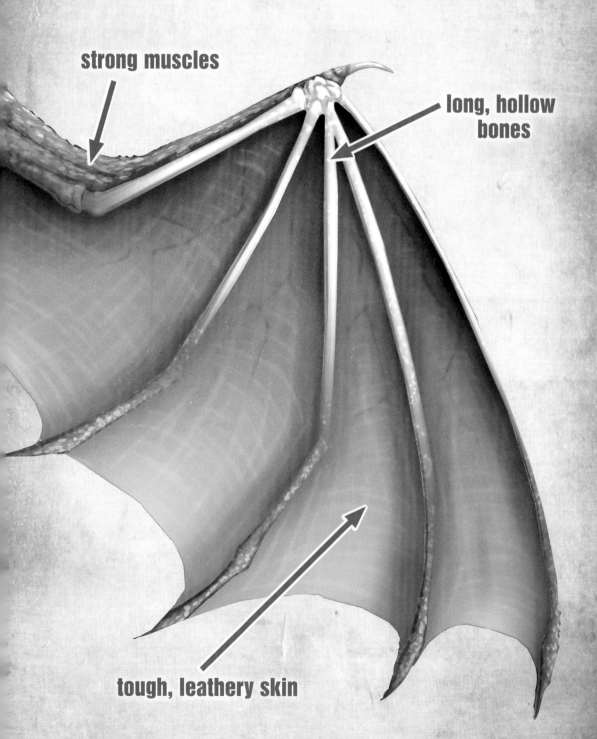

strong muscles

long, hollow bones

tough, leathery skin

19

BORN FOR BATTLE

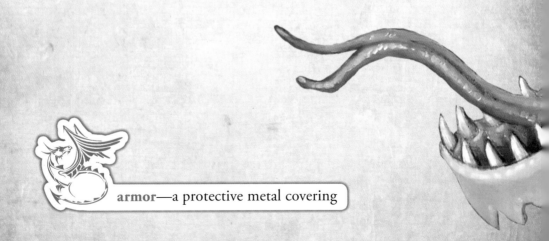

Dragons in most stories have several natural weapons. Dragons can easily bite through a knight's armor. Their mouths are filled with long, sharp teeth. And their powerful jaws can snap shut like a steel trap.

armor—a protective metal covering

DRAGON FACT

In some stories, people create deadly knives and other weapons from sharp dragon teeth.

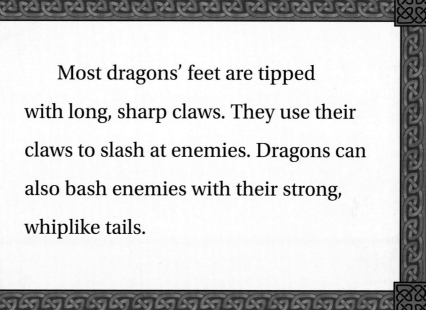

Most dragons' feet are tipped with long, sharp claws. They use their claws to slash at enemies. Dragons can also bash enemies with their strong, whiplike tails.

DRAGON FACT

Some four-legged dragons have thumbs on their front feet. They can use weapons and other objects just like people can.

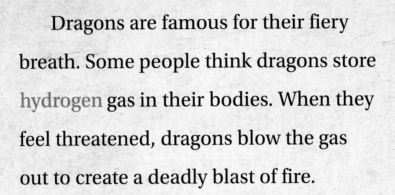

Dragons are famous for their fiery breath. Some people think dragons store hydrogen gas in their bodies. When they feel threatened, dragons blow the gas out to create a deadly blast of fire.

DRAGON FACT

Dragons don't get burned when they breathe fire. A thick layer of mucus protects their mouths.

hydrogen—a colorless gas that is lighter than air and burns easily

Not all dragons breathe fire. A frost dragon's breath quickly freezes anything it touches. Dragons in some stories may spit acid or venom. Others may have no breath weapon at all.

venom—a poisonous liquid produced by some animals

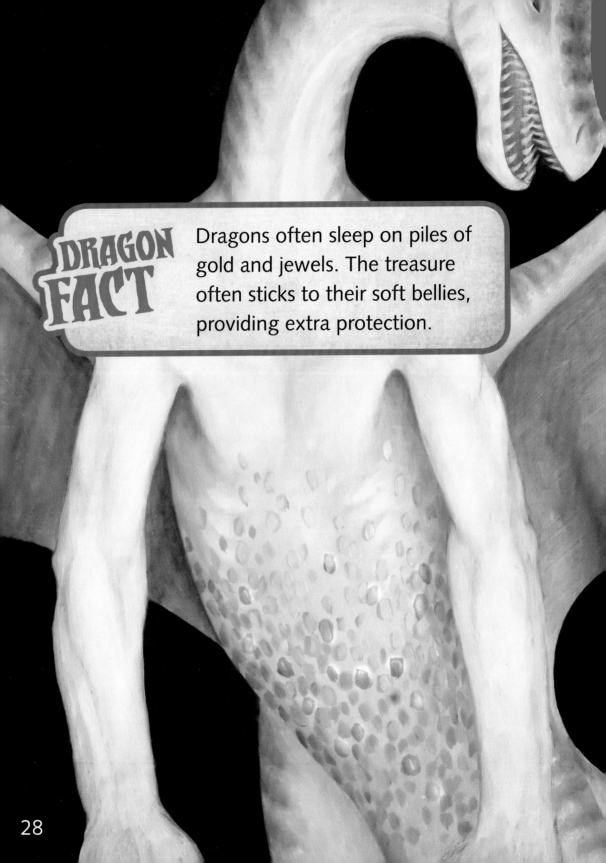

DRAGON FACT

Dragons often sleep on piles of gold and jewels. The treasure often sticks to their soft bellies, providing extra protection.

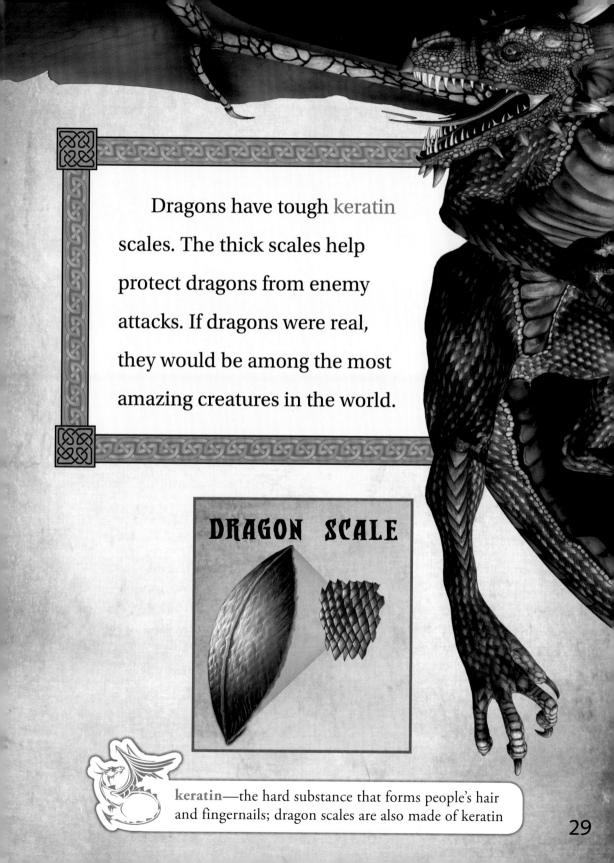

Dragons have tough keratin scales. The thick scales help protect dragons from enemy attacks. If dragons were real, they would be among the most amazing creatures in the world.

DRAGON SCALE

keratin—the hard substance that forms people's hair and fingernails; dragon scales are also made of keratin

GLOSSARY

armor (AR-muhr)—a protective metal covering

hydrogen (HYE-druh-juhn)—a colorless gas that is lighter than air and burns easily

Jacobson's organ (JAY-kuhb-suhnz OR-guhn)—an odor-detecting organ inside the mouths of some reptiles

keratin (KAIR-uh-tin)—the hard substance that forms people's hair and fingernails; dragon scales are also made of keratin

knight (NITE)—a warrior of the Middle Ages (AD 400–1500) who wore armor and fought with a sword

lair (LAIR)—a place where a wild animal lives and sleeps

mucus (MYOO-kuhss)—a sticky or slimy fluid that coats and protects the inside of the nose, throat, lungs, and other parts of the body

myth (MITH)—a story told long ago that many people believed to be true

scale (SKALE)—one of the small hard plates that covers the skin of some reptiles

skeleton (SKEL-uh-tuhn)—the bones that support and protect the body of an animal

venom (VEN-uhm)—a poisonous liquid produced by some animals

vibration (vye-BRAY-shuhn)—a fast movement back and forth

Read More

Caldwell, S. A. *Dragonworld: Secrets of the Dragon Domain.* Philadelphia: RP Kids, 2011.

McCall, Gerrie. *Dragons and Serpents.* Monsters and Myths. New York: Gareth Stevens Pub., 2011.

O'Hearn, Michael. *Sea Monsters vs. Dragons: Showdown of the Legends.* Monster Wars. Mankato, Minn.: Capstone Press, 2012.

Internet Sites

FactHound offers a safe, fun way to find Internet sites related to this book. All of the sites on FactHound have been researched by our staff.

Here's all you do:

Visit *www.facthound.com*

Type in this code: 9781620651452

Super-cool stuff! Check out projects, games and lots more at
www.capstonekids.com

INDEX